Getting Started with Golang Concurrency Primitives

Table of Contents

Chapter 1. Introduction

Welcome to this comprehensive Special Report, designed to guide you through the adventure of unraveling concurrency in Golang. In this report, we'll dive deep into Golang's concurrency primitives and explore how they empower developers to write efficient, scalable software. While the subject can seem dense and complex to newcomers, this report demystifies Golang's concurrency model in an approachable, digestible manner. The journey might be challenging at times, but rest assured, by the end of this specially curated report, you'll be armed with the knowledge and confidence to conquer the world of Golang concurrency. So, gear up and get ready to level up your understanding of Golang concurrency primitives, one page at a time!

Chapter 2. Getting Acquainted with Golang and Concurrency

Golang, also known as Go, is an open-source programming language that offers excellent support for handling multiple concurrent tasks. It's inspired by the likes of C, but consists of better abstractions, readability, and simplicity.

2.1. Just the Go Facts

Let's explore some quick facts about Golang. Go was designed at Google by Robert Griesemer, Rob Pike, and Ken Thompson. It is static typed and compiled, leading to highly efficient executable programs. It is equipped with a rich standard library and features built-in concurrency, which is its main attraction. The language is platform independent and can run on Windows, Linux, Unix, and MacOS systems.

2.2. Concurrency and Parallelism: Untangling the Terms

When we talk about concurrency and parallelism, we often use these terms interchangeably. But, in the world of programming, they entail different meanings. Concurrency revolves around independently executing processes meanwhile or interspersed. The processes might or might not be running at the same instant. It's about dealing with a lot of things at once.

On the other hand, parallelism involves executing multiple tasks at the same exact moment. It's about doing a lot of things at once.

Parallelism is impossible without concurrency, but concurrency doesn't always translate to parallelism.

2.3. Concurrency in Golang

Go is inherently designed to support concurrency. It is structured around the concepts of goroutines and channels, which we'll delve into in the subsequent sections. Go's design allows it to handle a large volume of concurrent tasks with ease, hence providing the advantage of optimizing processing speed and performance.

2.4. Exploring Goroutines

A goroutine is a lightweight thread managed by the Go runtime. It's like a regular function that runs concurrently with other functions. They are cheaper than threads as they take up less resources and can be created and destroyed with less overhead.

To create a goroutine, we use the 'go' keyword followed by the function call.

```
go f(x, y, z) //f, x, y, z can be any function and its
parameters
```

In this case, f will run concurrently with its caller.

2.5. Understanding Channels

Channels are a powerful feature in Golang that allow different goroutines to communicate with each other and synchronize their execution. Think of channels as conduits or pipes through which goroutines exchange data.

To create a channel in Go, we use built-in 'make' function.

```
ch := make(chan int) //creates a channel of integers
```

Data can be sent and received from a channel using '←' operator.

```
ch <- v    // Send v to channel ch.
v := <-ch  // Receive from ch, and assign value to v.
```

2.6. The Power of Go's Concurrency Approach

Handled correctly, Golang's concurrency approach is like a superpower. It allows developers to write efficient programs that make excellent use of the machine's hardware, tailoring to maximum performance and speed. The built-in primitives promote a model that encourages good practices, coherent design, and excellent performance.

2.7. Challenges in Go's Concurrency Model

While concurrency in Go empowers developers, it also brings along its fair share of challenges. Concurrency in Go can quickly become complex and hard to manage if we are not careful.

In conventional procedural code, you just have to worry about what your program does next. But with concurrent programs, managing and coordinating the order of operations between concurrent tasks becomes a whole other ordeal. It's like playing multi-dimensional chess where every move could affect many others.

Moreover, sharing memory between goroutines can also lead to race conditions — a situation when two or more goroutines access and manipulate the same data at the same time. The outcome then is dependent on the sequence of execution, making it unpredictable and leading to unintended consequences.

2.8. Final Thoughts

Understanding Golang and its concurrency primitives is the first stepping stone to unlock the power of concurrent programming in Go. While the road might seem perilous to newcomers, don't despair. With knowledge and practice, you'll soon grow comfortable with goroutines and channels. Moreover, understanding the challenges can help you navigate around potential pitfalls and mistakes.

Up next, we'll dive deeper into working with goroutines and channels, discussing their properties, syntax, and use cases. We'll explore patterns of concurrent programming and share best practices for tackling challenges in Go's concurrent model. Armed with this knowledge, you'll be ready to conquer the world of Golang concurrency, one goroutine at a time!

Chapter 3. Introduction to Goroutines

The core of Golang's concurrency strategy is the goroutine — a lightweight thread managed by the Go runtime. When executed, goroutines run independently alongside other goroutines in the same address space.

3.1. Understanding Goroutines

Just as you can't truly comprehend a language without understanding its grammar, recognizing the anatomy and semantics of goroutines is crucial to mastering concurrency in Go. As soon as a Go program is initiated, a single goroutine is automatically invoked, referred to as the main goroutine. Developers can spawn additional goroutines using the keyword go before function calls.

A simple parallel can be drawn with the typical main() function.

```go
func main() {
    fmt.Println("Hello, world")
}
```

If we intend to run the same fmt.Println() function in a new goroutine concurrently, we employ the go keyword.

```go
func main() {
    go fmt.Println("Hello, world")
}
```

In the second program, we create a new goroutine and the fmt.Println() statement is executed parallel with any consecutive

6

statements (if present) in main().

It's essential to recognize that once the function (in this case, main())
has finished executing, all goroutines running within that scope will
cease, even if they haven't completed their tasks.

3.2. The Lightweight Nature of Goroutines

Unlike traditional threads, which usually take up around 1MB of
stack in memory, goroutines are impressively light, often requiring
as little as 2KB. They're lightweight because the Go runtime contains
a scheduler that coordinates the execution of goroutines. This design
choice represents the heart of what makes Go's model of concurrency
shine. By extracting the management of thread-like structures into
the language runtime itself, Go can efficiently juggle thousands — or
even millions — of goroutines simultaneously without crippling
system resources.

3.3. Goroutines vs. Threads

At their core, goroutines and threads are the tools languages give
programmers to run code concurrently. However, they differ in
significant ways. Even though they both allow multiple activities,
threads are heavy and are managed by the operating system (OS),
whereas goroutines, being lighter, are managed by Go's runtime —
the core of a Go executable that manages memory, garbage
collection, and, importantly in this context, goroutines.

The other critical difference relates to cost and performance. Threads
are expensive, often consuming large chunks of memory, and
switching between them requires significant CPU work — a context
switch. On the other hand, since goroutines are less resource-
intensive and switching between them is managed internally by the

Go scheduler, it's both cheaper and faster.

3.4. Coordination Between Goroutines

To efficiently coordinate work between multiple goroutines, Go utilizes channels. Channels offer a way for goroutines to synchronize execution and communicate by passing a value of a specific type.

Imagine goroutines as workers in a factory, and channels as conveyor belts connecting them. Each worker (goroutine) operates independently of the others but uses the conveyor belt (channel) to pass parts (values) to the next worker. All the while, the factory manager (Go scheduler) overhead watches to ensure that operations continue smoothly and efficiently.

3.5. A Word of Caution

While goroutines are a powerful tool, as with any powerful tool, they must be used with care. Spawning unnecessary goroutines can lead to complications in code comprehension and maintenance. Additionally, goroutines come with their own caveats like goroutine leaks, which occur when goroutines are left hanging - not allowed to complete their execution and also not being recycled by the garbage collector. These leaks can eventually cause an application to run out of memory. Thus, thoughtful and judicious use of goroutines is advised.

This forms the prelude to a fruitful journey into Golang concurrency. This understanding of goroutines should give you a base to stand on as we venture forward. The forthcoming sections will unravel the interplay between goroutines and channels, zeroing in on various synchronization techniques, along with examples to illustrate all these concepts. This report will fuel further understanding and engagement with the magical world of Golang concurrency.

Chapter 4. Communicating with Channels

In the realm of Golang concurrency, channels play a pivotal role. Often likened to conduits or pipes, channels provide a way to communicate between concurrent goroutines. From data transfer to synchronization, channels empower complex yet manageable communication protocols, and give meaning to the idiom in Go that states, "Don't communicate by sharing memory, share memory by communicating".

4.1. The Basics of Channels

To create a channel in Golang, we use the built-in `make` function followed by the `chan` keyword and the type of the elements that the channel will handle. An example of this is shown below:

```
ch := make(chan int)
```

This code snippet creates a channel that can transfer integers. You can think of `ch` as being a pipe that can transport integers from one goroutine to another.

An important aspect to note here is that channels are strongly typed, just like variables. The type of the data that a channel can pass is fixed when it is created. Thus, a channel of type `chan int` can only pass integers.

4.2. Sending and Receiving from Channels

To send a value into a channel, we use the channel operator ←. For example:

```
ch <- 1
```

This code sends the integer value 1 into the channel ch.

On the other side, to receive a value from a channel, we can also use the ` ← ` operator.

```
value := <- ch
```

By using this code, we get a value from the channel ch and store it to the value variable.

4.3. Unbuffered Channels

By default, channels are unbuffered. When a value is sent into an unbuffered channel, the send operation blocks until a goroutine receives the value. This is a key point when working with Golang concurrency, because it allows goroutines to synchronize without explicit locks or condition variables.

In the following example, we launch a goroutine that sends the value 1 into the channel. The main goroutine blocks until it receives the value 1:

```
ch := make(chan int)
```

```
go func() {
    ch <- 1 // send the number 1 into the channel
}()

fmt.Println(<-ch) // receive and print the number 1 from
the channel
```

4.4. Buffered Channels

While unbuffered channels are great for synchronization purposes, sometimes it's useful to allow a sender to proceed without waiting. This is achieved with buffered channels.

A buffered channel has a queue of elements. The length of the queue is defined when the channel is created, and it determines how many elements a sender can send to the channel without being blocked.

For instance, in the example below we create a buffered channel that can store up to two integers:

```
ch := make(chan int, 2)
```

The sender will only be blocked when the queue is full. Similarly, a receiver will be blocked when the queue is empty.

4.5. Closing Channels

Sending to a closed channel causes a panic. To avoid this, channels can be explicitly closed by using the close function:

```
close(ch)
```

A Receiver can test whether a channel has been closed by performing a receive operation:

```
v, ok := <-ch
```

If ok is false, the channel has been closed and there are no more values to receive.

Keep in mind, closing channels is only necessary when the receiver must be notified there are no more values coming, such as to terminate a range loop.

4.6. Select Statement

The select statement allows a goroutine to wait on multiple communication operations. It's like a switch statement, but for channels. This can prove useful when dealing with various channels and operations.

```
select {
case v1 = <-ch1:
    fmt.Printf("Received %v from ch1\n", v1)
case v2 = <-ch2:
    fmt.Printf("Received %v from ch2\n", v2)
}
```

Conclusively, channels are an incredibly powerful tool in Golang. They provide a means to pass data between goroutines in a safe and concurrent manner, but they also introduce flow control and synchronization capabilities. Mastering channels surely means you've embarked on the path of grasping the beauty and power of Golang's concurrent model.

Chapter 5. Understanding Buffers in Channels

To embark on the journey of understanding buffers in channels, we must first grasp the concept of channels themselves. Channels can be thought of as pipes through which we can send and receive values with the operator ←. By default, these sends and receives block until the other side is ready, providing a convenient way to synchronize concurrent goroutines without explicit locks.

5.1. What are Buffers in Channels?

Unlike regular channels, buffered channels take a second parameter when you create them, which specifies the size of the channel buffer.

Here's an example to illustrate the creation of buffered channels:

```
ch := make(chan int, 5)
```

In the code above, we've created a buffered channel of integers that can hold up to five values.

Buffered channels are similar to regular or unbuffered channels, but they have an intrinsic capacity. The number provided to the make function indicates the capacity of the buffer. This allows the channel to hold that many values in it without a corresponding receiver for those values.

5.2. Understanding How Buffered Channels Work

Let's consider the same example:

```
ch := make(chan int, 5)
```

In this case, we're able to send five values on the channel without blocking. The channel only blocks on send once these five slots get filled up.

Let's see this play out in the following piece of code:

```
ch := make(chan int, 5)

ch <- 1
ch <- 2
ch <- 3
ch <- 4
ch <- 5

// The send below will block since the channel is
already full
ch <- 6
```

When we attempt to send the sixth integer value, the send operation will block because the buffer is full. For the send operation to proceed, there must be a corresponding receive.

5.3. Unblocking a Buffered Channel

Unblocking a buffered channel can be achieved in a couple of ways.

This could be done either by having a goroutine waiting to receive from the channel or by having a buffering policy in place.

For example, imagine a restaurant where the chef is serving food and the waiter is receiving the food that has been prepared. In our analogy, the foods prepared by the chef are the values that are sent on the channel, the waiter is the goroutine that is ready to receive from the channel, and the buffer can be likened to the counter where the chef places the food.

When the waiter is ready to receive (the chef has prepared food and put it on the counter), the chef can serve one of the meals on the counter, freeing up a space for more cooked meals. This represents a receive operation which allows a send operation to unblock and make a space in the buffer.

However, if the chef repeatedly tries to serve meals while the counter is full and the waiter is not ready to receive, this will lead to blocking because there's no space for additional meals.

5.4. Buffer Overflow and Buffer Underflow

When discussing buffered channels, concepts of buffer overflow and buffer underflow can be often encountered.

Buffer Overflow: In terms of Go channels, a buffer overflow situation occurs when we attempt to send more values to the channel than its capacity without a corresponding receive operation. As seen in the previous examples, this results in a blocked send operation.

Buffer Underflow: In the case of buffer underflow, it's when we attempt to receive from an empty channel, resulting in a blocked receive operation.

The appropriate handling of buffer overflows and underflows is crucial to the correct operation of a program.

5.5. Conclusion

The concept of buffered channels in Go provides a powerful way of synchronizing concurrent goroutines. It's an essential component of Go's concurrency model. By allowing you to specify the amount of data that can sit in channels before blocking occurs, buffered channels offer greater flexibility when coordinating tasks between goroutines.

However, these benefits come at the cost of increased complexity. Properly synchronizing goroutines can be a challenge, especially in larger applications. While unbuffered channels automatically sync goroutines, with buffered ones you will need to make sure your sends and receives align with the state of the buffer.

Understanding buffer overflow and underflow scenarios, and correctly implementing policies to deal with these cases, is key to leveraging the full potential of buffered channels. It's an exciting journey and an enriching experience to tame channels' buffers and harness their power to write more efficient, concurrent applications in Go.

As is true for any learning journey, mastering Go's concurrency model, of which buffered channels are an integral part, requires patience, practice, and resilience. We hope this chapter provided you with some clarity on buffers in channels and made your trip through the terrain of Go concurrency a bit less arduous.

Chapter 6. Locking Mechanisms: Mutex and RWMutex

Concurrency is a common challenge that developers face when writing software, and multi-threading makes it even more present. Go handles this through a variety of synchronization primitives, two of the most critical being Mutex and RWMutex, aimed at bringing order and predictability to a potentially chaotic computational world.

6.1. Working With Mutex

Go's 'sync' package provides a Mutex, a mutual exclusion lock type. The zero value for a Mutex can be used immediately, and it doesn't need to be initialized explicitly. Two methods can act on Mutex: 'Lock' and 'Unlock'.

```
// Declare a Mutex
var mutex sync.Mutex

// Lock
mutex.Lock()

// Unlock
mutex.Unlock()
```

Mutex's 'Lock' method allows a goroutine to gain exclusive access to a shared resource, blocking any other goroutine trying to acquire the lock.

The 'Unlock' method, on the other hand, releases the lock, allowing other goroutines waiting for the lock to acquire it. It's essential to ensure a locked Mutex gets unlocked correctly, as failing to do so creates deadlocks—situations where execution can't progress due to two or more goroutines waiting for each other to release a resource.

6.2. Deadlocks and Deferred Unlocking

Deadlocks are a common problem when working with Mutex, and Go's 'defer' statement is a helpful tool in avoiding them. With 'defer', you can postpone the execution of a function or method until the surrounding function returns, ensuring the Mutex is always unlocked.

```
// Lock Mutex
mutex.Lock()

// Make sure to unlock in the end
defer mutex.Unlock()
```

By putting the 'Unlock' operation inside a 'defer' statement directly after the 'Lock', you guarantee an always-executed 'Unlock', even if the method or function has multiple points of return or encounters a panic.

6.3. Mutex's UseCase

A typical use case for Mutex is protecting data access in a multi-threaded environment. Suppose you have multiple goroutines attempting to modify a shared variable. To prevent race conditions, a Mutex can be used as locking mechanism ensuring only one goroutine alters the data at a time.

```
// shared data
var counter int

// mutex
var lock sync.Mutex

// Update counter function
func UpdateCounter() {
    lock.Lock()
    defer lock.Unlock()
    counter++
}
```

Each goroutine trying to increment the counter will lock access to the variable, increment it, and then unlock it. Thus, the shared variable 'counter' is safe from concurrent modification.

6.4. Working With RWMutex

In scenarios where a resource is more often read than written, constantly locking and unlocking it for each read operation could lead to performance overhead. For optimizing such read-heavy operations, we have RWMutex in Go's 'sync' package.

A RWMutex (read-write Mutex) maintains a pair of locks, one for read access and the other for write access. Multiple goroutines can read the data in parallel but an exclusive lock is required for writing.

Methods associated with RWMutex are 'RLock', 'RUnlock', 'Lock', and 'Unlock'. 'RLock' locks for reading, 'RUnlock' unlocks from reading, 'Lock' locks for writing, and 'Unlock' unlocks from writing.

```
// Declare a RWMutex
var rwMutex sync.RWMutex
```

```
// Lock for reading
rwMutex.RLock()

// Unlock from reading
rwMutex.RUnlock()

// Lock for writing
rwMutex.Lock()

// Unlock from writing
rwMutex.Unlock()
```

Go's 'sync' package also offers the 'RLocker' method, returning a 'sync.Locker' interface implemented by the 'RWMutex', consisting of 'Lock' and 'Unlock' methods which lock and unlock the mutex for reading. This is particularly useful when the same RWMutex needs to be passed around for read and write operations.

6.5. Dealing with Starvation

However, RWMutex appears to have a problem—it suffers from the potential for starvation. Starvation occurs when a goroutine is unable to proceed because the resources it needs are constantly being given to other goroutines. In the case of RWMutex, if read operations are continuously arriving, write operations are starved since RWMutex gives priority to readers.

Unfortunately, Go doesn't provide a direct way to deal with the starvation problem in its RWMutex implementation. To overcome this limitation, you will either need to build your own synchronization structure that eliminates or mitigates the problem, or use a third-party library offering such a feature.

Mutex and RWMutex are simple, powerful tools to achieve thread safety in your complex applications, ensuring your Go code executes smoothly and efficiently. By mastering these concurrency primitives, you'll be one step closer to conquering Golang's concurrency model.

In our next exploration, we will wade further into the world of Go's synchronization primitives, tackling the powerful and versatile channels. But that is for another section. For now, be content and explore the power of Mutex and RWMutex—it's a lot to absorb, to experiment, and to implement.

Words of wisdom: Always release a lock (either on Mutex or RWMutex) you acquire, and use Go's defer feature to guarantee lock-unlocking, minimizing the possibility of a deadlock.

Chapter 7. The Sync Package: WaitGroups & Once

Concurrency is a powerful tool that Golang provides to its programmers. It opens up a whole new world where multiple tasks can be executed simultaneously, to enhance the efficiency and speed of our applications. To safely manage this realm, Go provides the sync package. This package exposes several types and functionality that allow for more advanced control of concurrent execution in Go code, mainly - WaitGroups and Once.

Let's start by understanding WaitGroups.

7.1. WaitGroups

WaitGroup is a struct type provided by the sync package in Golang. It is used to wait for the program to finish all the goroutines associated with the WaitGroup. This is achieved by maintaining a counter in the WaitGroup. When a new goroutine starts, the counter is incremented and when a goroutine finishes, the counter is decremented. The main goroutine waits for the counter to hit zero, indicating all the associated routines have completed.

The following is the definition of the WaitGroup type in the sync package.

```
type WaitGroup struct {
    state1 [3]uint32
}
```

This struct type comes with three methods Add, Done and Wait.

- Add: This function increments the WaitGroup counter by the value passed to it.

- Done: This function decrements the WaitGroup counter by one.

- Wait: This function pauses the execution of the goroutine in which it is called until the WaitGroup counter becomes zero.

Let's learn how to use WaitGroup with the help of an example.

```go
package main
import (
    "fmt"
    "sync"
    "time"
)

func worker(id int, wg *sync.WaitGroup) {
    defer wg.Done()

    fmt.Printf("Worker %d starting\n", id)

    time.Sleep(time.Second)
    fmt.Printf("Worker %d done\n", id)
}

func main() {
    var wg sync.WaitGroup

    for i := 1; i <= 5; i++ {
        wg.Add(1)
        go worker(i, &wg)
    }

    wg.Wait()
}
```

This code spins up five worker goroutines and waits for them all to complete.

7.2. Once

In the sync package, there is also the Once type that provides the ability to execute something just once. The struct Once has a single method Do, which accepts a function. The cool thing about the Do function is that, no matter how many times it is called, the function passed to it will only be called once.

Let's see 'Once' in action:

```go
package main
import (
    "fmt"
    "sync"
)

var once sync.Once

func performAction() {
    fmt.Println("Performing Action")
}

func main() {
    for i := 0; i < 10; i++ {
        once.Do(performAction)
    }
}
```

Even though once.Do(performAction) is called ten times, the performAction function is only executed once. This becomes important when you need to ensure that a particular task, such as initializing a variable or resource, is only done once in your program, regardless of the number of goroutines that might attempt the action.

7.3. WaitGroups vs. Once: Choosing the Right Tool

Both WaitGroups and Once allow us to manage goroutines in Go but they serve different purposes and should be used in different scenarios.

WaitGroups are the tool of choice when you need to wait until a set of goroutines have all completed their work. It provides an easy way to orchestrate and manage the execution of multiple independent goroutines.

On the other hand, Once is used when you want to make sure that a particular piece of code is only executed once, regardless of how many times it is called or how many goroutines call it. This can be useful in scenarios where you have some sort of initialization code that should only be run once.

In conclusion, understanding and leveraging the power of the sync package can significantly improve the performance and safety of your Go concurrent programs. Understanding when and how to use WaitGroups and Once, while dealing with concurrent programming, will allow you to write more efficient, secure, and maintainable code.

In the next section, we'll discuss Mutexes, another important feature provided by the sync package. Like WaitGroups and Once, Mutexes play a crucial role in letting us control and manage concurrency in Go, especially in scenarios where shared data resources are accessed from various goroutines. That is a story for another day, though. For now, practice and become proficient with WaitGroups and Once. Happy coding!

Chapter 8. Exploring Concurrent Data Structures

Let's start by exposing the problems inherent with shared data in a concurrent context—a certain understanding of which is required to fully appreciate concurrent data structures.

8.1. Understanding Data Races

When multiple goroutines manipulate shared data, we often fall into the unfortunate pitfalls of **data races**. A data race occurs when two or more goroutines access the same variable concurrently and at least one of them performs a write operation. This often leads to unpredictable results, causing programs to behave nondeterministically. Consider an inappropriately guarded increment operation:

```
[source,Go]
----
var counter int
var wg sync.WaitGroup
```

```
func main() {
    for i := 0; i < 1000; i++ {
        wg.Add(1)
        go func() {
            defer wg.Done()
            counter++
        }()
    }
    wg.Wait()
    fmt.Println(counter) // Output: ???
```

```
}
----
```

In the above case, the counter is shared among multiple goroutines, with each executing the increment operation on it. The result of the program will indeed be nondeterministic and probably lesser than the expected 1000 due to the existence of data races.

8.2. Solving Data Races

Solving data races involves designing a mechanism to orchestrate the access to shared data. Golang offers several methods, two of which are - Mutex locks and Channels.

1. **Mutex Locks: Mutex** or **mutual exclusion** is a standard mechanism used across various programming languages to control the access of shared resources to avoid conflicts. In Go, `sync.Mutex` or `sync.RWMutex` can be used to guard shared data.

   A modified and fixed version of the previous program using a mutex lock could look something like this:
   ```
   [source,Go]
   ----
   var counter int
   var wg sync.WaitGroup
   var mtx sync.Mutex
   ```

   ```
   func main() {
       for i := 0; i < 1000; i++ {
           wg.Add(1)
           go func() {
               defer wg.Done()
               mtx.Lock()
   ```

```
        counter++
        mtx.Unlock()
      }()
   }
   wg.Wait()
   fmt.Println(counter) // Output: 1000
 }
 ----
```

Here, the `counter++` operation is guarded by
`mtx.Lock()` and `mtx.Unlock()`. This ensures that
only one goroutine can increment the counter at a
given time, effectively eliminating the data race.

2. **Channels:** Another way to avoid data races is to use Channels
   that allow you to pass the ownership of data from one goroutine
   to another. Channels encourage a style of programming where
   you don't have to worry about locks as data is not shared and
   thereby, eliminates the data races.

8.3. Introducing Concurrent Data Structures

We now understand the problems with shared data in concurrent
programming and how to resolve data races in Go. Concurrent data
structures are an extension to these concepts.

Concurrent data structures are data structures designed to be used
by multiple goroutines, which can read from and write to the
structures efficiently. They are designed keeping in mind that
multiple operations on the data structure can be executed
simultaneously. They use mechanisms like locks or channels inside
the data structure to prevent data races.

Go does not offer built-in concurrent data structures. We are often compelled to use traditional data structures with appropriate guard mechanisms to ensure safe concurrent access.

8.4. Concurrent Data Structures: Maps

Let's take a closer look at how to make traditional map data structures concurrent in Golang.

A map in Go is a built-in data type that associates keys to values. However, when they are read/written by multiple goroutines simultaneously, they can lead to a data race. Here, Mutex locks come to our rescue, allowing us to handle concurrent reads/writes in a map.

```go
type ConcurrentMap struct {
    sync.RWMutex
    items map[string]int
}

func (cm *ConcurrentMap) Set(key string, value int) {
    cm.Lock()
    defer cm.Unlock()

    cm.items[key] = value
}

func (cm *ConcurrentMap) Get(key string) (int, bool) {
    cm.RLock()
    defer cm.RUnlock()

    value, ok := cm.items[key]
    return value, ok
```

```
}
```

Here, the `sync.RWMutex` allows multiple goroutines to read a resource without any nasty effects of data races but requires exclusive access during write operations.

This just scratches the surface of Concurrent Data Structures in Golang. We'd discussed an approach to fortifying maps for concurrent use. Similar strategies can be applied to other data types as per requirements. Beyond this, you may come across patterns and strategies focused on optimizing read/write operations for better performance in specific scenarios.

Remember, concurrency is a powerful tool but can add complexity to your code. Therefore, always be sure to balance the cost against the benefits when implementing it. And always remember the Go proverb: "Do not communicate by sharing memory; instead, share memory by communicating."

So, embrace the robust and efficient parallel computation capabilities of Golang, and make the best out of them for your software development needs!

Chapter 9. Concurrency Control Patterns

Concurrency in Golang offers an efficient way to handle multiple tasks at a time, and contributes significantly to performance optimization. More precisely, it is a way to structure software, particularly as a way to write clean, understandable code that interacts well with the real world. The power to harness concurrent computing fully lies in understanding and effectively using the control patterns it supports. In this report, we will investigate a few primary concurrency control patterns used in Golang: Channels, Mutual Exclusion with `sync.Mutex`, Lock-Free concurrency using `sync/atomic` package, and the `sync.Cond` for Conditional Variables and `sync.WaitGroup` for wait groups.

9.1. Channels

A core aspect of concurrency in Go is the Go Channel. Channels provide a way for two goroutines to synchronize execution and communicate by passing a value of a specified element type.

Create a channel with the built-in `make` function, and the syntax is `make(chan type)`. For example, `make(chan int)` creates a channel that can pass integers. Sending and receiving data from the channel isn't possible until the other side is ready. This behavior allows goroutines to synchronize without explicit locks or condition variables.

Code Example:

```
chnl := make(chan int)
go func() {
    chnl <- 1  // send a value to the channel
}()
```

```
val := <-chnl  // receive a value from the channel
```

9.2. Mutual Exclusion with 'sync.Mutex'

Concurrency control commonly involves coordination to prevent concurrent modification of shared data, causing a race condition. In Go, this is achieved using mutual exclusion i.e., sync.Mutex.

A Mutex is a mutually exclusive flag. It protects access to shared data by locking and unlocking data. If one goroutine holds the lock on a Mutex, any other goroutine that attempts to acquire that lock will block until it's released.

Code Example:

```
var mutex sync.Mutex
var counter int
go func() {
    mutex.Lock()
    counter++
    mutex.Unlock()
}()
```

Lock and Unlock control the access to the shared resource. It's crucial to balance operations on a mutex: for every Lock call, there should be a corresponding Unlock in the same goroutine else it'll result in a deadlock.

9.3. Lock-Free concurrency with 'sync/atomic' package

Lock-Free programming is a method where you manage shared, mutable state without the need for blocking synchronization primitives like mutexes. The sync/atomic package provides atomic memory primitives which allow lock-free synchronization.

Code Example:

```
var counter uint64
go func() {
    atomic.AddUint64(&counter, 1)
}()
```

The AddUint64 function automatically adds a number to counter without the need for a lock. It's faster and more scalable than mutex but only use it when you can express your algorithm as simple atomic memory operations to avoid data inconsistency.

9.4. Conditional Variables with 'sync.Cond'

Sometimes, our program needs to wait not only for a particular goroutine to complete but for a specific condition to become true. Here, conditional variables in the form of sync.Cond come into play.

Code Example:

```
var sharedRsc = make(map[string]string)
var m = sync.Mutex{}
var c = sync.NewCond(&m)
```

```go
go func() {
    m.Lock()
    sharedRsc["rsc1"] = "foo"
    c.Signal()  // notify the condition has met
    m.Unlock()
}()
m.Lock()
for len(sharedRsc) < 1 {
    c.Wait()  // wait for the condition
}
val := sharedRsc["rsc1"]
m.Unlock()
```

9.5. Wait Groups with 'sync.WaitGroup'

When handling concurrent execution, another challenge is to wait for all goroutines to complete before proceeding. This process is eased by 'sync.WaitGroup'. When creating goroutines, add a counter using wg.Add(1). Then, wg.Done() can signal the completion of a goroutine.

Code Example:

```go
var wg sync.WaitGroup
wg.Add(1)
go func() {
    // some work here
    wg.Done()
}()
wg.Wait()
```

The concurrency control patterns in Golang are powerful tools that allow developers to manage concurrent operations easily. Understanding these patterns will enable you to build capable and performant Go applications. Each has its use-cases, advantages, and shortcomings. Therefore, deciding on when to use each pattern comes with experience and a solid understanding of the problem at hand.

Chapter 10. Handling Errors in Concurrent Programs

As you venture into concurrent programming in Golang, one crucial aspect that you can't ignore is error handling. Concurrent programming, due to its nature, presents certain challenges when dealing with errors that might not arise in a simple, single-threaded context. In this section, we'll explore these challenges and present you with techniques to overcome them.

10.1. Understanding the Nature of Concurrency-Related Errors

Concurrency, the ability of a program to perform more than one task simultaneously, is what makes Golang a prime choice for high-traffic applications. However, it comes with certain types of errors that are often rare and elusive in a sequential programming paradigm. These errors can emerge from the smallest details and often depend on specific timing patterns or random events, making them hard to reproduce and challenging to debug.

Consider, for example, race conditions – when the behavior of a system depends on the relative timing of events. This type of error can cause intermittent failures, making them especially tricky to address. Deadlocks—a state in which each member of a group of actions is waiting for another member to release a lock—is another concurrency-specific error. Such errors can result in system-wide failures which are not easy to recover from. So, having knowledge of these kinds of mistakes is paramount to building solid concurrent programs.

10.2. The Traditional Error Handling Mechanism in Golang

Golang has a straightforward error handling mechanism. Functions generally return an 'error' as the last return value. If an operation was successful, the error will be 'nil'. However, if there was a problem, the error will contain information about what went wrong.

```
func Foo() (int, error) {
    return 0, errors.New("an error occurred")
}
```

However, this traditional mechanism often falls short when dealing with concurrent operations, as you might end up with multiple return values representing different errors. Moreover, identifying which particular concurrent operation the error originated from becomes a nontrivial task.

10.3. Handling Errors in Goroutines

Goroutines, the lightweight threads managed by Golang, are at the heart of its concurrency model. They allow your program to perform tasks concurrently, leveraging multiple processor cores. However, this also means that they can fail separately and require a strategy to handle such errors effectively.

Here's a simple way to handle error from a Goroutine using a channel:

```
func worker(errs chan<- error) {
    if somethingWrong {
        errs <- errors.New("something wrong occurred")
    }
```

```
    // Rest of the function
}
```

In the above code, we pass an error channel to the worker function running in a Goroutine. If an error occurs during execution, it's sent over the channel. Elsewhere in your program, you can listen on this channel and handle errors accordingly.

10.4. Enhancing Error Handling with Packages

Golang's standard library is a powerful tool, but for advanced error handling, you might need to rely on third-party packages. The 'pkg/errors' package, for instance, allows you to wrap errors with more context, providing a stack trace that can be incredibly helpful for debugging.

```
import "github.com/pkg/errors"

func worker(errs chan<- error) {
    if somethingWrong {
        errs <- errors.Wrap(errors.New("something wrong
occurred"), "worker")
    }
    // Rest of the function
}
```

Here, if an error occurs in the worker function, it gets wrapped with a message before being sent to the error channel. The message "worker" provides additional context to the error.

10.5. Adopting the Pipeline Pattern for Error Handling

The pipeline pattern is a typical pattern in concurrent Golang programs. You have a series of stages, each stage is a group of Goroutines, and each such group has specific tasks assigned. They are connected via channels, forming a pipeline: output from one stage is the input to the next.

In such a pipeline, one robust way to propagate errors is by having a dedicated error channel at each stage. If any worker encounters an error, it sends the error into this channel, terminating its execution. The receipt of an error from this channel can be used to signal a shutdown for the entire pipeline.

10.6. Leverage Context for Error Handling

The context package in Go is another critical tool for managing errors in concurrent programs. When you have a bunch of Goroutines, and one of them encounters an error that should halt all others, a great way to propagate this halt signal is by using a Context.

The Context package in Go is designed to enable the transfer of deadlines, cancel signals, and other request-scoped values across API boundaries and between processes. It's particularly useful to fail an entire network of Goroutines when any of them encounter an error.

10.7. The Art of Error Recovery

The 'recover' function provided by Golang is a special built-in function that regains control of a panicking Goroutine. It can be a helpful tool in specific cases where errors should not cause the whole program or a significant part of it to crash.

To conclude, error handling in concurrent programming with Golang is a critical skill for writing robust and resilient applications. The traditional error handling mechanism might need to be expanded upon, but Golang's rich set of tools and language constructs make it possible to navigate this challenging territory efficiently.

Chapter 11. Concurrency in Action: Real-world Examples

Concurrency is one of the foundational pillars of Golang, inspired by Tony Hoare's Communicating Sequential Processes (CSP). Concurrency semantics in Go provide a convenient and powerful approach to manage parallelism, achieving high performance and scalability. In this chapter, we'll look at concrete, real-world examples of concurrency in action using Golang.

11.1. Real-World Example 1: Parallelizing CPU-Intensive Tasks

One pivotal benefit of concurrent execution is the ability to parallelize CPU-intensive tasks, enabling responsive, high-performance applications. Consider an image processing scenario where the task is to convert RGB images to grayscale images.

The naive, non-concurrent approach might look something like this:

```
func grayscaleImage(image Image) Image {
    // ... convert image to grayscale ...
}

func convertImages(images []Image) {
    for _, image := range images {
        grayscaleImage(image)
    }
}
```

In the above code, images are processed sequentially. If each image takes one second to process and there are 1000 images, the function would take around 1000 seconds to execute. Here's where Go's concurrency shines.

```go
func grayscaleImage(image Image, result chan<- Image) {
    // ... convert image to grayscale ...
    result <- grayImage
}

func convertImages(images []Image) {
    result := make(chan Image, len(images))
    for _, image := range images {
        go grayscaleImage(image, result)
    }
    for range images {
        fmt.Println(<-result)
    }
}
```

In this revised version, converting each image is a separate goroutine, capable of running concurrently. By deploying this approach, we can significantly speed up the execution time by leveraging multi-core processors.

11.2. Real-World Example 2: Improving I/O Intensive Tasks

Go's concurrency primitives are also splendid for I/O intensive tasks. Consider an application that needs to fetch pages from multiple URLs.

Without concurrency, we might end up with this kind of code:

```go
func fetchPage(url string) string {
```

```
    // ... fetch page ...
}

func fetchPages(urls []string) {
    for _, url := range urls {
        fetchPage(url)
    }
}
```

With each fetch being a blocking operation, this code would be quite slow. Thankfully, we can introduce goroutines and channels to achieve concurrent execution:

```
func fetchPage(url string, result chan<- string) {
    // ... fetch page ...
    result <- pageContent
}

func fetchPages(urls []string) {
    result := make(chan string, len(urls))
    for _, url := range urls {
        go fetchPage(url, result)
    }
    for range urls {
        fmt.Println(<-result)
    }
}
```

Again, each fetch operation is now a separate goroutine, freeing the application to execute other tasks during I/O waits.

11.3. Real-World Example 3: Worker Pool Pattern

A common real-world use case is the worker pool pattern. This pattern is useful in controlling the number of goroutines in execution, providing a way to throttle CPU or I/O consumption. In a usual scenario, we spawn a set of worker goroutines and distribute the work among them via a channel.

```go
func worker(tasks <-chan Task, wg *sync.WaitGroup) {
    defer wg.Done()
    for task := range tasks {
        // ... process task ...
    }
}

func processTasks(tasks []Task) {
    taskChannel := make(chan Task, len(tasks))
    var wg sync.WaitGroup
    for i := 0; i < workerCount; i++ {
        wg.Add(1)
        go worker(taskChannel, &wg)
    }
    for _, task := range tasks {
        taskChannel <- task
    }
    close(taskChannel)
    wg.Wait()
}
```

The `sync.WaitGroup` primitive, in this case, helps in ensuring all goroutines finish executing before allowing the main goroutine to proceed. Notice how we use the channel to pass the tasks to the workers and the close function to indicate that no more tasks are coming, a common pattern in Go.

These are just a few real-world examples demonstrating the power of Go's concurrency model. Concurrency in Go provides a great foundation to build high-performance applications and services. As we immerse ourselves in Go, we'll continue to explore these concepts in detail, gaining insights into buffered channels, select statements, and more nuanced facets of Golang's concurrency story. As the saying goes, "Don't communicate by sharing memory; share memory by communicating." Happy coding!